My Brother is Different is a book about Autism in the most unconventional sense. This book is not about the Autistic child per se. Its focus is on the sibling of the Autistic child, the so-called "normal" child. The book is a valuable guide to help families cope with the overwhelming feelings and fears experienced by the "normal" child.

The book is two-sided; Part I is for the parents. It deals honestly with the effect their Autistic child is having on their other child, the normal one. It provides straight talk and a unique perspective about a difficult subject.

In Part II, parents turn the book over and begin to read the book with the normal child. Parts II and III are written from a child's perspective with accurate illustrations, which support the realistic subject matter. The thoughts and feelings of the sibling are shared through his eyes.

Finally, Part III becomes a vehicle for acceptance through positive affirmations that replace negative thoughts with positive, reinforcing statements. It helps children accept and cope with their life while reinforcing parental love. It resounds with the affirmation, *MY BROTHER IS DIFFERENT, BUT THAT'S OK, I LOVE HIM ANYWAY!*

For CMM
For believing in me,
Forever and Always.

No work would be complete without a list of those
individuals who helped me along the way.

To my children, Sheila and Scott, my first treasures.
You are my inspiration.
For Chloe and Cooper, my latest blessings.
To Mike for his devotion.

To my brother Larry, who pushed me for 20 years
to "Write it already!"

~ BJM

My Brother is Different

A parents' guide to help children cope with an Autistic sibling

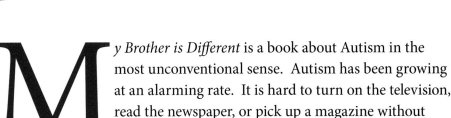

My Brother is Different is a book about Autism in the most unconventional sense. Autism has been growing at an alarming rate. It is hard to turn on the television, read the newspaper, or pick up a magazine without finding Autism featured.

On a daily basis, families are trying to cope and are bombarded with information. Yet, there isn't much out there about the normal child in the household, the child witnessing the family in crisis.

This book is NOT about the Autistic child; it offers no theories or magic pills. Rather, it is a recipe to help families cope with the overwhelming feelings, fears, and everyday life as experienced by their normal child. It will assist the parent with acknowledging fundamental yet painful truths while assisting their normal child cope with the life he or she lives.

PART I

The book is two-sided; Part I of the book is for you, the parent. It deals honestly with the reality of life and the effect your Autistic child is having on your other child, the normal one. This section explains the basis for the book and identifies its purpose. By dealing with the fundamental issues, it states in plain language how you got here, what is really happening in your life, and how you can help your normal child. It presents the difficulties rarely discussed about the child who is often forgotten but tremendously affected by his or her Autistic sibling. It provides straight talk and a unique perspective about a difficult subject. It details how parents can sometimes forget the emotional needs of their normal child. It reviews the range of emotions that floods the mind of the normal child in a straightforward manner. Negative thoughts played over and over in the mind become real and frightening to a child. Sometimes their young minds can't put their thoughts into words, yet they feel bad. They can feel anger, guilt, and shame. By addressing these issues with your child and reading them aloud you give your child a powerful message. You begin to control the situation and slowly replace his or her negative feelings with positive messages. Since the majority of Autistic children are males, I have chosen to call the Autistic child in this book, "my brother."

PARTS II AND III

Part II of the book should be read to your normal child. It is written at a child's level with simple illustrations that provide accurate visual support of this difficult subject. In terms that children will understand, it addresses their fears and negative emotions. It is written from the child's point of view. Bottled-up thoughts and negative emotions are brought out in the open. After this section is completed, the next portion of the book is read. This section, Part III, can stand alone, as its own independent book. Initially, it must be read as a partner to Part II. However once Part II is read and openly discussed a few times (you be the judge of how many), important lines of communication are established, and reviewing this section will no longer be necessary.

Part III of the book contains powerful affirmations that replace negative thoughts with positive, reinforcing statements that help the child cope. They become aware that their feelings are normal; everyone has bad thoughts from time to time. They learn that they are valued and loved and that their parents are not angry with them. It helps the child realize that he or she is not responsible for their sibling's problems or behaviors. This section may be read over and over to remind and reinforce positive messages. It will help them with their anxiety and fears. You, as the parent, will help them learn how to cope with their feelings and their life. Learning to accept their situation and find peace is such an important life lesson. You will help your child work on this goal.

PARENTS' PORTION OF *MY BROTHER IS DIFFERENT*

No one goes into parenthood looking for problems. We go with hopes and dreams. The journey as a parent begins when you first learn that you are pregnant. You are excited, happy, and perhaps fearful and concerned. You go through the long nine-month period of waiting. Finally, the long awaited day comes; the baby finally arrives! Wow, you never saw anything so small. He has all his fingers and toes and appears perfect. You are in love. The wonder of that tiny baby who gurgles and cries and needs you is awe-inspiring. You are grateful for his health, his robust appetite, and even his piercing cry. You go home and begin your new life as a family. You have hopes and dreams for your little one. You feel blessed. As you look into his

2

eyes, you see his bright future. His tiny fingers grasp yours, and you feel so responsible for this little bundle of life. Life with a newborn is chaotic and a blur. The baby grows and seems to thrive. All is well.

Around eighteen months to two years, you begin to feel that something isn't quite right. You are not sure. You go to doctor, your baby is examined, and all seems okay. But . . . you just know something is wrong. They say he seems fine; just wait and watch. You are told to give it time and relax. So you do. Later, there are more doctors, more questions, more worry, and more fear. Perhaps it is at age three that your child gets the diagnosis, for some later, for some earlier. Regardless of when you hear the words, the feelings of devastation are there.

Your child is Autistic, there is no cure. It is a lifelong challenge. There is no magical pill, no magical therapy. Each child is unique; what works for some does not work for others. These are harsh words but true. The road to find the right mix of intervention, therapy, and education is rocky and fraught with battles. But you already know that. Since Autism is a diagnosis that has a huge spectrum of related disorders, children manifest the symptoms in varied ways.

WHAT WE KNOW

Autism is the fastest growing developmental disorder in the United States.

The areas that may be affected are:

- Behavior
- Communication
- Cognition
- Social Skills

AUTISM MAY BE CALLED:

- Autistic Disorder
- Pervasive Developmental Disorder (PDD)
- Pervasive Developmental Disorder Not Otherwise Specified (PDDNOS)
- Asperger's Disorder

OTHER FACTS

- Autism appears in the first three years of life.
- Children may be diagnosed up to age five.
- Autism is four times more prevalent in boys.
- There is no medical test for Autism (such as, a blood test, tissue sample, or urinalysis).
- There is no cure for Autism.
- There are many theories of the causes but no definitive answers.
- There are many questions with no simple or direct answers.
- Some children with Autism have little or no cognitive impairment.
- Some children may have mild to severe cognitive impairment.
- There are varying degrees of Autism.
- Children have behaviors that are unique to them.

CHARACTERISTICS

There are a multitude of behavioral characteristics that Autistic children may develop. Some children demonstrate many of the characteristics and some may have just a few. The following list is neither inclusive nor exclusive. It is simply a guide to the most typical behaviors.

The Autistic child may demonstrate:

- limited social interaction
- limited eye contact
- dislike of physical contact
- a lack of awareness of their environment
- a lack of awareness of others
- a delay in speech or have limited speech
- limited understanding of spoken language
- limited use of language
- repetitive behaviors, such as finger flapping, rocking, spinning, clapping
- the need for routine, may become upset if routine is changed
- walking on tiptoe
- fascination with certain objects
- eating issues, a dislike of certain foods because of color or shape

The Autistic child may also:

- repeatedly line up toys, cards, any object in a specific way
- have issues with clothes, shoes, etc.
- perseverate on certain objects, such as a clock, buttons, zippers, shoelaces, etc.
- have a short or long attention span
- have severe temper tantrums
- have self injurious behaviors, such as head banging; finger, hand, or nail biting; hair pulling, etc.
- have severe atypical responses to their environment
- overreact to noise, visual stimuli, or people
- not like crowds, close spaces, elevators, escalators
- have excessive fears of objects, places, etc.
- have cognitive impairment or cognitive limitations

"Autism can be treated, with the right intervention. Some children may learn to handle their behaviors, and can learn to live with Autism."

How did this happen to your child? You listen to what the experts say. They say that Autism is the fastest growing developmental problem in the United States. It is also growing at an alarming rate in Europe. So you go on, you research, you learn, and you live each day. You do not have the answers. No one has all the answers. You learn as you go along. This is how the saga begins for many parents of Autistic children. The painful journey has just begun. This book recognizes that painful and difficult time and provides help and an approach you can use with your normal child.

So here we are now. You are ready to read this book. In your heart you know why. Know? Know what? You know that your normal child is suffering and you are too tired, too worried, all used up with thoughts and energy spent on your Autistic child; the child, who needs so much, requires so much care, nurturing, energy, effort, and attention. You feel guilty, so guilty. You know you should give your normal child more . . . more time . . . more of you, but you just can't right now.

You made a good choice; you are reading this book.

You realize that there is something that must be done. Congratulations! You have just taken the first step to help you normal child reach emotional wellbeing. Right now, you are beginning to make a change. Let's begin the journey together. You will learn how to help your normal child achieve some emotional and psychological peace. Dealing with normal children can be a pleasant and wonderful experience. We will work with his or her thoughts, and fears and validate them as great children. It will pay off now and throughout your child's lifetime.

Working in the field of Special Education for the past 36 years, I have had so many conversations with parents of disabled children. I have heard so many stories; heart wrenching ones as well as joyful ones. I have counseled parents, told parents truths they were not prepared to hear, and laughed and cried with them. Some families never got over their bitterness and hurt, never made it through the grieving process. What about the grieving process? Parents of children with any type of disability all experience the grieving process.

THE GRIEVING PROCESS: WHAT IS IT? WHY IS IT RELEVANT?

Grief is defined as great sorrow. Any major life-changing loss, such as the death of a loved one, a severe trauma, a debilitating illness, etc., can cause grief. Since it so commonly associated with death, why is it mentioned here? Because a discussion about grief belongs here. Parents who have a disabled child grieve. It is a normal reaction to a major loss. In this case, it is the loss of a child, the healthy normal child. Instead they have an Autistic child, an unanticipated outcome. This situation is so new and so frightening. When the diagnosis is made, it can throw the family into the grieving process overnight. The family is in chaos. Since grief is a process not an event, it takes time to work through it. There are no set time limits. In the case of a disabled child, parents may grieve for years. It is widely accepted that *The Grieving Process* has multiple stages. Individuals go through the stages of grief at their own pace. Not everyone will go through all of the stages. Some families work through it; some get stuck and can't work their way through it.

THE STAGES OF GRIEF

- **Denial and Shock**
- **Anger**
- **Bargaining**
- **Guilt**
- **Depression**
- **Loneliness**
- **Acceptance**

Denial and Shock

At first, you find it difficult to accept the reality of having an Autistic child. You deny the diagnosis or feel that perhaps something else may be wrong with your child. You are fearful and insecure and can't believe that it can be true. You are overwhelmed.

Anger

You are angry! You feel that it is unfair. Why your child? Why has this affected your family? You may loose your temper with others, the doctor, and the teachers. You may verbally lash out at professionals trying to help. You don't want to hear it. Your anger may help you cope.

Bargaining

You try to make a deal with a deity. You will give something up "if only" your child would be well. You will exchange your health, money, education, etc., for your child to be "normal."

Guilt

You feel guilty. Maybe it is your fault. You should have been more careful, you should have followed a better diet during pregnancy, you should have relaxed more, exercised more, and so forth. Shoulda, woulda, coulda, whatever. Nothing you could do could change things. Yet, you feel so responsible. You feel guilty; it makes you sick. You feel responsible, therefore you feel guilt.

Depression

You have experienced a great loss. You are filled with sorrow. You feel isolated and may experience hopelessness. Some parents say they have a "walking" depression. They take care of things but are profoundly sad. You may feel empty inside and just seem to go through the motions, but you feel disconnected.

Loneliness

Your life has changed so drastically. Your time is filled with caretaking activities. You don't go out. You feel isolated and alone. There is no time for a social life.

Acceptance

Finally you reach acceptance. You may still not be happy with your circumstances, but you accept where you are and try to make the best of it. You begin to deal with the reality of the situation and feel like you are gaining control. Eventually you reach a point where you can see the light at the end of that tunnel. You have learned how to move on from the pain and look to the future with hope and positive goals.

Grief can be physical as well as emotional. Parents experience the loss of their child. They yearn for the child they lost; the child that was well, the child that was normal. Grieving is a normal reaction to extreme emotional pain. You have had significant pain. It is real, it is powerful, and it is your reality.

Why do parents grieve? They grieve for what could have been, what should have been. They grieve for themselves, and they grieve for their child. They grieve for lost hopes and dreams. They grieve for the present and grieve for the future their child will not have. They grieve out of love and grieve out of fear. Grief can be consuming and bottomless. Some make it through the process and get to the final stages of grief to acceptance and hope. Some never get there. Acceptance may take years. Some parents never get over their bitterness. They play the blame game and hold on to their anger like a shield. I have helped many families through this process; many are grateful and accepting. Others are still working it out, dealing with pain, disappointment, and anger. Their lives are tough. Having an Autistic child changes the family dynamic FOREVER. It is life altering yet can also be filled with joy.

If you feel that you need help in dealing with your grief, you may find a support group very helpful. Talking and sharing with other parents of Autistic children may help. There are no easy answers in dealing with your grief. Grieving is a slow process. Please allow yourself the time to grieve, it is normal and necessary. It is important to talk about your feelings, seek out family or friends or professionals if needed. It is essential to learn how to cope with your feelings.

Eventually, you will find your way out of your grief. You will begin to find pleasure in the simple joys of living. You will learn to find satisfaction in your Autistic child's accomplishments, however small. You must allow yourself to feel happiness and delight. One of the essential elements of acceptance is to learn to laugh at yourself and find humor in situations. Laughing at yourself helps you to cope. Look at your glass as half full rather than half empty. Your attitude controls your reality. Choose to be positive; it is contagious. It is all in your perspective. Your situation will be the same, but your positive perspective can make all the difference. Don't miss the joys in your life by carrying around the burden of grief. Negativity sucks the life out of you.

WHAT IS *MY BROTHER IS DIFFERENT* ABOUT?

This book is NOT about Autism in and of itself; it is about how the Autistic child affects his or her normal sibling. It is NOT about you, the parent. It is NOT about your choices of therapy, education, and so on. It will NOT provide advice about the current trends and intervention. It will NOT discuss the pros and cons of childhood immunizations and whether it is the right or wrong thing to do for your child. There are numerous books and sources out there about these topics. Talk to the medical experts about immunizations; you will not find that advice here.

This book is about your OTHER child, the normal one. The child who has on his or her shoulders all your hopes and dreams for success. Or perhaps you forget about this child's emotional needs because you are so busy. Well, he or she is there, quietly observing, listening, and hurting. Ok, so this upsets you and rightfully so. The truth is that your normal child is hurting in ways you cannot believe. The purpose of this book is to help this child. I am not saying that you are a bad or neglectful parent. You are not. You are overwhelmed, exhausted, and hurting; your life has changed. You did not choose this; there just isn't anymore of you to go around. If your time were to be depicted as a pie, all of the slices would be portioned out with nothing left for you. This is understandable. You are taking care of your child's basic needs; food, clothing, and shelter; the child is safe. But there is so much more you need to do. This book is meant to be a guide for the parent to deal with the normal child's emotional and psychological needs. It will open up important lines of communication. It is necessary to share more information with your normal child. It is necessary to hear what he or she is thinking. It will be hard for you to read some of the child's thoughts out loud, but, it will pay off.

You are the most important person in your child's life. You can have a positive impact on how your child responds to what he or she sees and hears. You have taken an important step. You acknowledge that things need to improve and know that they must.

You know in your heart that you are not giving the same level of nurturing to your normal child. You know that your major focus is your Autistic child. You can't help it. Your Autistic child has placed a strain on you, your family, and your marriage. All of your relationships are suffering. You feel as if you have no life. You feel as if you have lost yourself. You can't remember when you last laughed or had fun. When was the last time you had a night out? You fight with your spouse or significant other. Caring for yourself is no longer a priority. You go through the motions of life but feel that you are not living. Sometimes you feel robotic. Well, if you feel like this, how do you think your normal child feels? After all, they are living in the same home. They are living and growing in this hopeless environment. They are too young to fully understand what is wrong but they know that something isn't right. They try to disappear or they become more demanding. They can withdraw or act out.

You have got to pay attention to these normal kids. The 800-pound gorilla in the room must be addressed and discussed. Sometimes parents perceive these quiet well-behaved normal kids as a godsend, grateful for their passive behavior. Well, many times puberty hits and watch out! These kids can unleash their wrath. Kids ignored or pressured to be perfect may sometimes do anything to get your attention. If they don't explode behaviorally they may implode. After all, negative attention is still attention. Many teens act out with drugs, promiscuity, or delinquency. Some teens shut down and become depressed and even more invisible. Just because they are quiet does not mean that they are okay. You must deal with them while they are still young so that emotional healing can begin. They need to be secure in your love.

When you read Part II of this book, it will begin to open honest communication between you and your child. By dealing with the essential issues, you begin a process that will continue for many years. This will create a positive relationship based on honesty, trust, and openness. The benefits will be significant for your child. He or she will feel that you are approachable. Your behavior will send the message that you are ready and able to handle his or her problems in a positive and meaningful way. You will deal with the 800-pound gorilla in the room. You will provide information about Autism and talk about your family's reaction to it. This gives your child the security of knowing that things are not perfect, but the family unit continues to try and deal with life the best way possible.

Bringing this subject up is just another hurtful reminder of just how difficult your life has become. It will not go away if we do not address it. The good thing is that you have already taken action. By reading this book you have made the decision to help your normal child. You are taking the important steps to help your child cope with their life. Recognizing the pain your child is feeling is important. It is very isolating for a child to have an Autistic sibling. They do not know how to process their feelings. They feel shame and guilt about their thoughts. Their life is also different. For example, you do not have the same type of family activities other families have. Birthdays and holidays may be celebrated differently. They may not have their friends over. You may not go out together to the movies or the mall. All activities outside of the house may have to be planned. Your child is aware of how different their life is compared to others. They know that they do not enjoy the same activities and events like other kids. It can build resentment in your child. But these children are too little to articulate this to you. They are hurting and feel like they are missing out because of an Autistic sibling.

They have scary thoughts they can't tell you, and they are ashamed. When negative thoughts are played over and over in the mind of a child,

they become frightened victims. These thoughts become so powerful. Sometimes their minds can't put their thoughts and feelings into words. They just feel real bad.

The purpose of the child's section of *My Brother is Different* is to rewrite negative thought patterns with positive affirmations and begin to change their thinking.

HOW TO USE PART II

Part II of the book should be read aloud to your normal child. While reading, you can observe their reaction and open up truthful communication. It will give you an opportunity to seek out their unique point of view. The first portion of the child's section addresses the real feelings of isolation, fear, resentment, and loneliness your child may have. By reading this out loud, you give your child a valuable message. You acknowledge that you understand and accept your child's feelings, however raw and difficult it may be. You accept their feelings and tell them that they are normal. Many of the thoughts expressed in this section can break your heart, but not recognizing them and discussing them is much worse, worse for your child and worse for you. When children keep their feelings bottled-up, their feelings gain even more power and may become toxic. The mere act of reading aloud addresses your child's feelings. They no longer have to keep their feelings secret, thereby releasing them from a terrible burden. You will tell them it is okay to have these feelings, it is normal. You are NOT bad. Every child with an Autistic sibling may have these thoughts from time to time. That is okay. Your thoughts and feelings are just things you feel and think. But they do not have the power to hurt. Sometimes these kids are so tormented that they cannot put their emotions into words. They are afraid; they feel guilty for thinking them. They may feel they should be punished. By reading them out loud and bringing them out in the open, children feel relieved. In this regard, you will be teaching them to cope. You clarify that "thoughts are just thoughts; you think them in your head. They are not actions, and they do not hurt you or your brother or sister."

Adults are not the only people who become depressed. Children under stress may also develop depression. It is important to recognize the symptoms so you may help your child when necessary. Children do not exhibit the signs of depression in the same manner an adult does. If you begin to see a real change in your normal child's behavior, pay attention. It may be temporary, or it may be more serious than that. If you notice your normal child exhibit the signs of depression you must seek out the medical experts. You must act, these behaviors will not go away, and will probably get worse. You should always begin with your pediatrician. Talk to him or her and explain what is happening. They may recommend a child psychologist or child psychiatrist. Please listen to your doctor. It is better to deal with it when they are young. Children sometimes need more help than a parent can provide. There is nothing wrong with getting professional help; there is no shame in this. The field of child psychology has grown; there are a lot of gifted professionals out there who can help your children. Get them help if they need it. It is the best thing you can do.

SIGNS OF DEPRESSION IN CHILDREN
- Changes in typical behavior
- Sadness or frequent crying for no reason
- Changes in eating and or sleeping
- Withdrawal
- Loss of interest in favorite activities
- Acting out behaviors (behavior changes)
- Trouble in school (not wanting to go to school)
- Difficulty focusing
- Unexplained physical problems
  (complaints about tummy ache, headaches)

It is my sincere hope that by dealing with the concepts outlined in this book, you can avoid the whole issue of childhood depression. We are trying to deal with emotional healing and honest communication. However, I would be remiss if I did not review depression and its effects on children. Therefore, it is included in this section as a guide if you need it.

THE *ESSENTIAL QUESTIONS* FOR PART II

Since the purpose of Part II is to open an honest dialogue. The following open-ended sample questions will assist you. Remember, you want your child to feel comfortable talking about his brother or sister. There are no right or wrong answers. The responses are simply your child's thoughts and feelings. You may respond with the following:

I see.

I understand.

I hear you.

Sorry, I didn't know.

I am listening.

You may also repeat what your child says to make sure you understand what he or she is telling you (e.g., You get upset when your brother hits himself, is that right?). This form of response provides assurance that you are listening carefully and understand what you child is saying. Always include one of these statements: "I am so glad you shared this with me," or "I am glad we had this talk." You need to provide a positive response to let your child know that you are not upset or angry. Feel free to add your own questions and responses.

This exercise opens up a universe of possibilities. It is important for your child to share this with you.

Please impress upon them that they are not judged by what they think but how they act. Their compassion for their sibling is what you see. Tell your child that he or she is very observant and caring and that you will work with him or her to manage any concerns.

ESSENTIAL QUESTIONS

- **Does your brother do some of the same things the boy in the book does?**

- **What other things does your brother do?**

- **When your brother acts in this way, how do you feel?**

- **What scares you?**

- **What makes you mad?**

- **What makes you sad?**

- **Tell me some things you wish we could do as a family?**

- **How are you and your brother alike?**

- **How are you and your brother different?**

- **How can mommy and daddy help you feel better?**

- **What kinds of things can we do?**

These are just some of the questions you can ask. The purpose is simple, you just need to get your child to talk. Your job is to listen carefully and remember how your child is feeling. Your goal is to help them feel better, safer, secure, and loved.

HOW TO USE PART III

The last section of the children's book, Part III, is what I call positive affirmations. Here you provide powerful positive messages. You affirm that they are good and caring. You affirm your love and acknowledge their thoughts. These affirmations, which you will read out loud, will provide a positive and accepting message of love and caring. This section of the book is critically important. It will provide a kind and productive response, which, when repeated, works to neutralize your child's negative thoughts.

Negative thoughts have real power over children; they feel shame for having them and are afraid of what your response will be when you find out. When children continually focus on negative thoughts in their minds, the thoughts become destructive. Your positive and accepting response will, over time, negate their fears and show them that you love and cherish them. Positive parental statements have tremendous power over children. Words can hurt, and words can heal. We can help your children heal by modifying their thoughts and encouraging them to believe in their good nature. This is not a quick fix; it is a process that, when read over time, will help your normal child cope with their Autistic sibling. Our goal is the same; we both want your children to be emotionally healthy and feel love and acceptance for themselves and their brother who is different.

This section of the book may be read independently after you have read the first section. It will not be necessary to always read Part II of the book. Once Part II is read and the message is absorbed, Part III may be read time after time to reinforce the positive message. Part II is just a vehicle to open lines of communication and get your child to talk about their feelings and fears. Part III is the final element of *My Brother is Different*. This section should be read repeatedly to remind your child of his or her worth. Remind them they are an important member in your family.

SO LET'S BEGIN . . .

Turn the book over and put your normal child on your lap, next to you, or wherever you are comfortable, and begin to read.

Flip the book over
and let's begin.

ABOUT THE AUTHOR

Barbara Morvay has been in education for 37 years. She began her career as a speech therapist and teacher of disabled children. She later became an administrator of special education as well as a principal of a special needs school. She recently retired as the superintendent of a school district in southern New Jersey, which specialized in the education of disabled children. Barbara has dedicated her entire career to helping disabled children and their families.

Illustrations By Lisa Confora
The illustrations in this book were rendered in watercolor.

Graphic Design By Jeanne B. Daubner

Pursuant to the Consumer Product Safety Improvement Act (CPSIA),
Printed in the United States
February 2010 • M7040
by BookMasters, Inc.
30 Amberwood Parkway
Ashland OH 44805

US $24.99
Canada $29.99
ISBN 978-0-9709582-1-1

For information or to order additional copies, visit www.mybrotherisdifferent.com

My Brother is Different
A sibling's guide to coping with Autism

PART II

This section should be read aloud to your child.

The purpose of **Part II** of this book is to open up important lines of communication.

Your normal child sees so much, yet they do not fully understand what they are seeing.

Sometimes the visual messages are interpreted incorrectly.

After reading this section you can openly discuss what was read.

The Essential Questions identified in the parent's section should be asked

after reading **Part II**.

My Brother

Me →

This is me, and this is my brother.

My brother is different.

I do not know why.

He looks the same as you and me.

It makes me want to cry.

My brother is not happy.

He doesn't laugh or play.

He doesn't like to smile.

I guess that's okay.

3

He has problems with so many things.

He is a very picky eater.

Eating is hard for him, you see.

He does not like to eat like you and me.

He doesn't eat food

that is round or yellow.

I wish he were a happier fellow.

He likes soft food, but doesn't eat much.

He likes to have spaces on his plate.

He doesn't like his food to touch.

Mealtimes are hard and there could be tears.

I just eat fast and climb the stairs.

My brother likes to hang upside down.

I don't know why, I just frown.

He gets mad and loses control.

Sometimes it's scary for me.

My brother can be really quiet.

He can just sit and stare.

8

He doesn't even know you are there.

My brother lives in his own world day after day.

I wonder how he got this way?

I hope I don't get like my brother.

It would scare me to be like him.

It's all about my brother, every day and every night.

9

I get sick of it, doesn't mommy see?

Sometimes I don't like him, it hurts me to say.

My brother only cares about himself.

How did he get this way?

I wish mommy would know just how upset I get.

I just don't know what to say or do.

I try to help my brother but nothing works.

I try and try, but I can't help him, so it hurts.

He doesn't want to play with others, you see.

My brother does not have any friends.

He does not seem to mind, so I guess it's okay.

The only thing my brother likes to do

is play with colored blocks the whole day through.

He lines them up the same way everyday.

If you touch them or try put them away,

he will throw himself on the floor and kick and scream.

You better not go near him when he acts that way.

My brother does the same thing again and again.

He doesn't get bored like you or me.

He doesn't like to sleep or have people visit.

My brother doesn't like toys, video games, or movies.

My brother doesn't care about holidays or cookies.

My family takes care of my brother so much.

I'm lonely and feel left out.

It seems that my parents forget that I am here.

My friends can't come over to play.

It's hard for people to see my brother this way.

Most kids don't understand a kid like my brother.

I wish I could have a birthday party.

I could have friends, balloons, a cake, and prizes.

I could be like the other kids and just have some fun.

But we don't have parties at my house.

So I won't ask because mommy will just say no.

My brother is different in so many ways.

He does lots of things other kids do not do.

I will try to explain them to you.

He rocks back and forth and doesn't say much.

He plays with his fingers, and he plays with his toes.

He hates haircuts and doesn't like clothes.

My brother doesn't like to go to bed at night.

So he screams and cries and makes a fight.

Sometimes he bangs his head until his forehead gets red.

I watch mommy try to calm him down.

Sometimes he hits her and pulls her hair.

I hate it, it's just not fair.

Bath time is hard for my brother and my mom.

My brother is afraid to take a bath, you see.

Water is scary to him but not me.

So I try to be good and not be a pest.

Mommy and daddy are tired.

They just need a rest.

My brother is funny about the clothes he wears.

He would stay in pajamas all day long.

He only wears soft clothes, no shoes, just sneakers.

He likes to walk in his bare feet and on his tiptoes.

Why he does this, nobody knows.

My brother doesn't know right from wrong.

When he is bad, he doesn't mean it, you see.

He doesn't understand like you and me.

My brother can get really upset, but he can't tell us why.

So sometimes he will just cry and cry.

Sometimes at night, I hear my parents fight.

Mommy cries and daddy gets upset.

I don't know what they say.

I can't help them anyway.

My brother doesn't know how hard it is for them.

I get scared and upset, too.

I just don't know what to do.

I wish things were different than they are right now.

I feel so alone with no one to talk to.

I think so many things in my head.

It is not nice, but I can't help it.

Do you think I'm bad?

If I were good, maybe I could make things better.

Mommy wouldn't cry and daddy wouldn't be sad.

Sometimes I think if my brother was not here,

we all could all be happy together.

I have to stop thinking bad things, it's not nice.

I wish we could go to places like my friends.

But, we stay home day after day.

We went to the mall once but it was a mess.

We were in a store,

when my brother threw himself on the floor.

He wouldn't get up, he started to cry and just threw up.

People just looked at us and I felt bad.

They just shook their heads and looked away.

It was a bad, bad day.

I got upset and wanted to cry.

I wished I was invisible and wanted to hide.

So we don't go out much as a family.

We don't want that to happen again, you see.

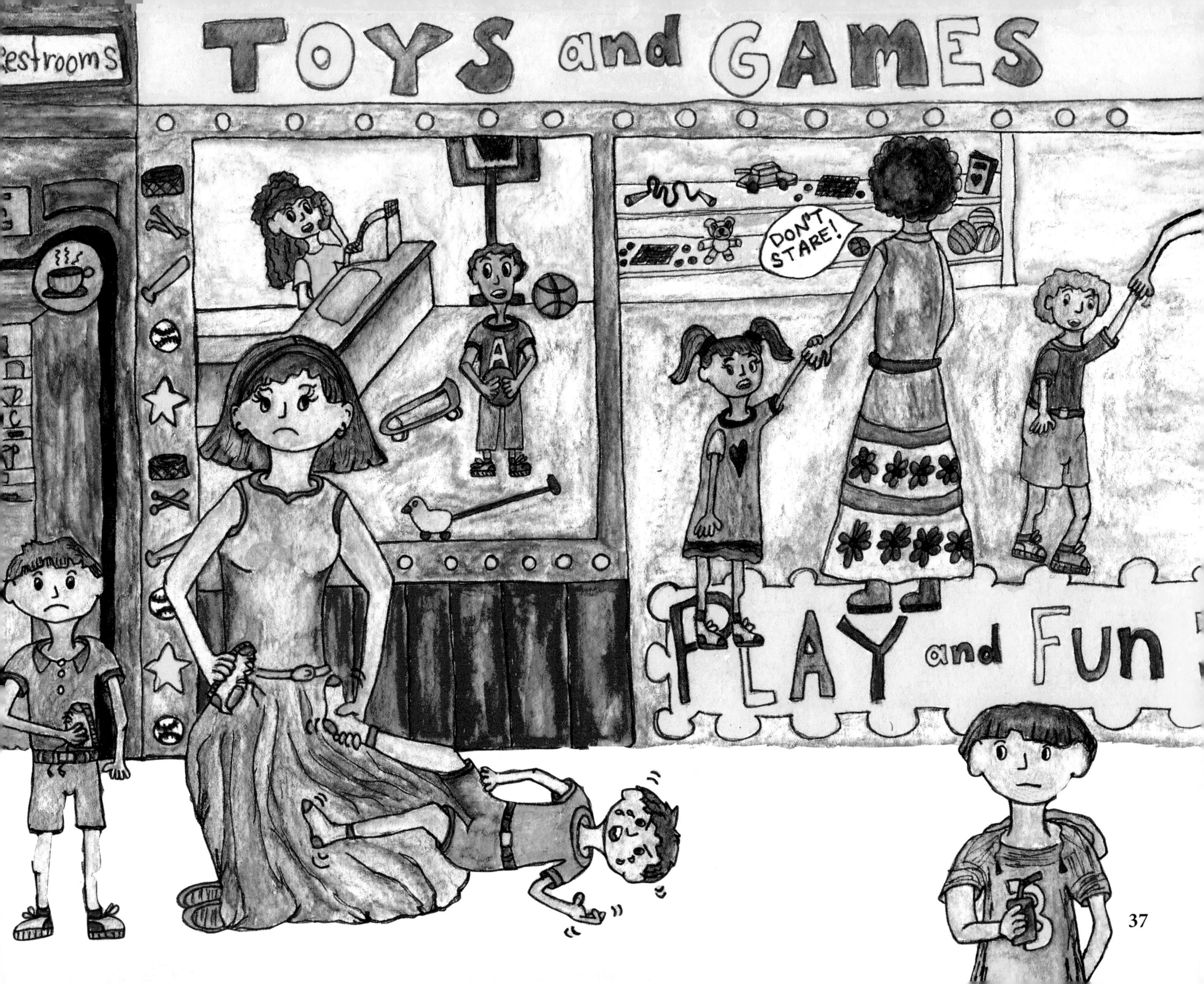

Restrooms
TOYS and GAMES
DON'T STARE!
PLAY and FUN

Aa Bb Cc Dd Ee Ff Gg Hh Ii Jj Kk Ll Mm Nn Oo Pp Qq Rr Ss Tt Uu

Longitude
Latitude

N
W——E
S

Multiply
X
2 X 3 = 6

Addition
+
2+2+2 = 6

Ms. Smith

← Me

I am happy when I go to school.

I am glad to be away from my house.

I make believe that I am like my friends,

just a regular kid with a normal family.

I feel that I have to be good all the time.

I can't upset my parents, they are sad already.

I worry all the time about our family.

I want to feel special and know my parents care.

I want us to go out and have fun together.

But we can't because of my brother.

Sometimes I think they love my brother more than me.

They spend all their time with him and not me.

I feel bad when I think these things in my head.

But I never say them out loud for anyone to hear.

I can't tell my parents, or they will think I am bad.

I really try to be good and always listen.

But sometimes I can't help it, and I get into trouble.

I am always feeling bad whatever I do.

My brother goes to the doctor a lot.

But the doctor doesn't ever make him better.

I guess he is just really sick. I feel so bad.

I hope I can't catch what he has.

But I don't say this out loud; I know better.

I try not to think bad things. But I just can't help it.

I can't tell my mommy, she will think I am mean.

So I try to be good, keep myself busy.

I stay by myself and try to be quiet.

I can help mommy and daddy by just being good.

I can try not to need them for anything.

I can help by making believe I am not here.

So mommy and daddy have more time for my brother.

He cannot help it, I know.

My brother is different and that's hard for me too.

Sometimes it is hard to fall asleep in my bed.

I start to think of all these things in my head.

I get scared of what I am thinking but can't tell.

Will I ever feel better and understand more?

My brother is different.

I know this is true.

because of him, my life is different too.

My Brother is Different

A sibling's guide to coping with Autism

PART III
Positive Affirmations

This section may be read alone or with Part II.
It may also be read independently after you have read Part II numerous times.
After discussing your child's issues, and depending upon your child's age,
you may provide additional information about Autism.
Give fewer details for the younger child and more information to the older child.

Your brother is different.

It affects our whole family.

We are going to talk about our situation.

We need to give you more information.

We will teach you things and start out slow.

It is up to you; tell us how fast to go.

Your brother is Autistic, this you know.

You cannot catch it, like a cold or the flu.

Your brother will be Autistic for the rest of his life.

He will learn to live with it and learn how to cope.

We must be strong and positive and always have hope.

53

54

Mommy and daddy are sorry, we just didn't know how you were feeling.

We feel bad we did not see that you suffered too.

We will try to explain as simple as we can.

Please stop and tell us if you don't understand.

We want you to see that we need you to learn

all the things about your brother you do not know.

We are sorry you felt lonely and sad.

We will try to include you so you won't feel bad.

He sees things and feels things but can't always tell us.

Many things that he does he cannot help.

He is learning how to handle his behavior.

It is a very slow process that takes a lot of time.

We need to praise him for things he does well.

He needs to know that we are proud of him.

He may try but fail at times.

Yet, we must encourage him to try again.

Learning new things is hard for him.

Just remember, your brother loves and needs you,

but he can't say the words.

Some of the things he does are behaviors

Autistic children do.

There are lots of Autistic children.

They do not all behave the same way.

He likes things to be the same every day.

He likes to have a routine; he feels safe that way.

ROUTINE means that he likes to do the same things the same way each day.

He gets scared of new things and doesn't like change.

Autistic children have many behaviors that are the same.

They may also develop their own way of acting.

We will try to explain as much as we know.

This will take time, but don't be afraid.

Mommy and daddy had to learn about Autism too.

Together we will try to make it easier for you.

We know that you have been scared, so let's make it better.

We will all learn together.

You can ask us anything; we won't mind.

Your feelings will not change what we think about you.

Mommy and daddy love you; you mean the world to us.

You are a great kid and try so hard.

Thank you for your good behavior.

We know that you think things in your head.

They scare you and make you feel bad.

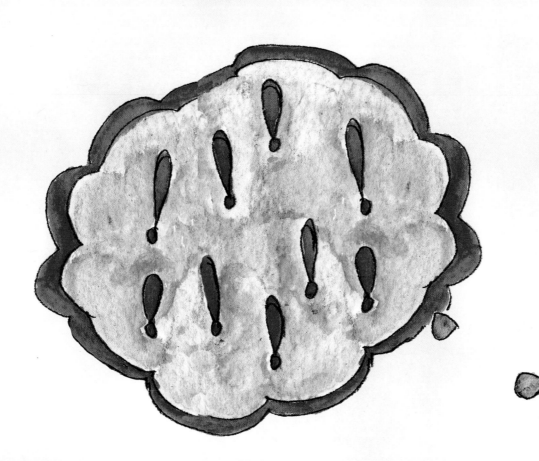

Thoughts that you have in your head are normal.

Everyone thinks all kinds of things.

Some things can make you feel awful!

But they are just thoughts and will go away.

Thoughts are just ideas that pop in your head.

They can be good, bad, funny, or dumb.

62

But thoughts have no power and can go away.

You will not be punished for the things you think.

Those thoughts are yours, and only you know what they are.

That's why we are talking so you understand.

When we talk about things it takes the fear away.

Because if you tell us we can help you feel better.

63

We know that you get scared.

We want to help you feel safe and secure.

Your brother is different, and that may hurt.

You are not responsible for his Autism.

Whatever you think cannot make him worse.

You are not bad for thinking these things.

Nothing you can think can change our love for you.

You will always be our child, and we will always love you.

Your brother needs assistance with everyday things.

He can't do them alone, so he needs our help.

Your brother gets lots of attention, that is true.

His Autism is no one's fault.

Just because we give your brother

so much time,

does not mean we love you any less.

We love both of our children

with all our heart.

We will try to give you

more of our time.

We will help you understand.

Together we will make

our family better.

We care about what you think
and what you feel.
You cannot keep everything inside.
Sharing helps you deal
with your fears.
We think you are a wonderful child.
We are going to tell you
just how special you are,
and how much
mommy and daddy love you.

So listen so you can hear.

We will tell you to say them out loud too.

Repeat after me, we want you to say it.

Please believe in yourself.

Here we go . . .

- I am a good brother.
- I am a great son.
- It is ok to feel bad, sometimes we all do.
- I will learn how to live with my brother and not get upset.
- I will share things that scare me with my mommy and daddy.
- I understand that feelings cannot hurt me.
- It is not my fault my brother is different.
- My brother is the way he is because he was made that way.
- I cannot catch his Autism.
- Mommy and daddy will always love me.
- They are proud of me no matter what.
- I will tell mommy and daddy if I feel bad.
- I will ask for help if I need it.
- We will talk about it so I can understand.
- We are a family and love each other.
- I will help other children understand my brother.
- My brother tries so hard to learn.
- My brother wants to be good.

I can help people understand,

that Autistic children just need more help.

My brother has changed my life,

in many positive ways.

I have learned about caring.

I have learned to help.

I have learned to listen.

I have learned to be patient.

I have learned to be kind.

I have learned how to LOVE.

There are a lot of brothers just like mine.

We all live in this world together.

My brother is different, and that's ok.

I LOVE HIM ANYWAY!

Me →

My Brother →